I0170899

Food

ESL Word Puzzles

Kathy Nosal

Misula Press

Orlando, FL

Printed in the United States of America

Cover photo credit: Unsplash

First edition published 2018

10 9 8 7 6 5 4 3 2 1

Nosal, Kathy

Just One Topic ESL Word Puzzles: Food ESL Word Puzzles / Kathy Nosal

ISBN-13: 978-0692850060

ISBN-10: 0692850066

Misula Press

Quote

"Food is our common ground, a universal experience."

-James Beard

Table of Contents

Word Puzzles and Vocabulary Activities

Learning New Words

Answer Section

Introduction

Word puzzles are a fun way to build your English vocabulary. This book will help you:

- Practice your food-related vocabulary
- Discover new food-related words
- Create a Vocabulary Notebook to learn new words
- Create a Pronunciation Page of words for speaking practice

These puzzles are a way to test your vocabulary skills and learn new words.

Here are some tips for doing the puzzles and activities.

- If a word puzzle is difficult, then stop doing that one and work on another puzzle. You can always go back and finish. Do not get frustrated; you are learning English!

- To make a puzzle more challenging, set a timer for 10 minutes (or any amount of time) to finish a puzzle.

If you want a fun way to test your vocabulary and learn new English words, then give these word puzzles a try!

Level: ESL High Beginning and up; this book is American English.

Word Puzzles and Vocabulary Activities

Word Search 1 – Foods

Goal: Word Searches help you learn new words and recognize the words you know.

Look at the list of words at the bottom of the page. Find these words in the boxes below. The words read forward or down. The word, *butter*, is an example of a forward word. The word, *egg*, is an example of a down word. Circle each word you find and then cross it off the list. Add words you do not know to your Vocabulary Notebook at the back of the book.

b	u	t	t	e	r	o	b	s	l	m	m	p	c	v	z	i	q	f	e
v	k	j	u	v	c	k	q	b	d	l	c	s	o	u	p	a	c	o	g
y	k	a	t	r	o	n	i	o	n	b	e	p	f	o	p	s	m	f	g
l	t	o	p	a	s	t	a	f	u	n	a	a	f	r	r	t	i	m	s
o	r	t	y	p	e	o	t	r	t	b	n	t	e	c	p	w	v	a	o
l	y	o	l	i	v	e	s	g	s	h	j	p	e	p	p	e	r	s	s
e	l	h	d	e	i	v	l	r	b	a	p	j	w	z	n	p	i	o	x
t	o	n	p	c	r	b	n	n	x	r	h	m	q	o	c	s	c	b	v
t	s	f	h	k	m	a	i	o	n	y	a	t	c	w	q	y	e	l	m
u	c	w	u	i	n	n	b	o	j	s	m	e	o	w	b	m	d	h	a
c	a	t	f	r	e	a	v	i	o	x	b	e	e	f	e	t	t	m	r
e	b	u	r	n	x	n	y	i	s	d	u	t	p	n	w	z	o	o	g
r	e	p	i	z	z	a	f	x	p	o	r	u	y	r	v	e	s	s	a
a	t	g	e	r	i	n	o	y	l	f	g	y	w	o	e	a	b	o	r
b	u	j	s	l	c	y	k	w	p	m	e	u	r	c	p	h	u	n	i
h	d	o	o	t	c	h	o	w	d	e	r	w	p	m	u	f	f	i	n
m	e	c	j	s	i	p	r	r	z	y	b	a	a	h	o	k	y	p	e
l	t	u	r	k	e	y	h	g	t	x	w	i	o	e	a	o	p	b	e
k	g	h	r	d	p	o	i	s	i	a	u	o	c	d	g	v	p	o	m
z	w	e	e	k	p	r	t	o	a	s	t	g	w	b	i	o	s	m	l

		Bonus Word
~~butter~~	turkey	The Bonus Word is not on the list. Find it using this hint.
onion	lettuce	
pasta	peppers	
soup	beef	
coffee	pizza	
chowder	rice	
toast	banana	**Hint**
~~eggs~~	nuts	It is something you eat for breakfast.
hamburger	margarine	
fries	olives	

Word Search 2 - Foods

Look at the list of words at the bottom of the page. Find these words in the boxes below. The words read forward or down. Circle each word you find and then cross it off the list. Add words you do not know to your Vocabulary Notebook at the back of the book.

l	y	p	n	v	t	o	b	v	l	m	m	p	x	h	e	r	b	s	g
d	e	j	u	v	c	k	q	e	d	l	c	k	f	e	e	a	c	o	k
y	k	a	t	r	p	e	v	g	u	i	e	p	v	o	p	s	m	f	o
l	s	o	m	a	s	t	a	e	g	n	j	a	t	r	s	t	i	m	t
o	h	t	i	p	e	o	t	t	o	b	e	t	u	c	o	w	v	a	o
h	r	o	l	l	s	x	t	a	l	h	l	x	a	i	d	o	t	s	s
s	i	h	k	e	i	v	l	b	b	a	l	j	b	e	a	n	s	o	x
t	m	n	p	c	p	c	n	l	x	r	y	m	q	o	c	s	m	b	v
i	p	f	h	k	i	i	b	e	u	t	e	t	c	w	f	r	u	i	t
m	c	w	u	i	n	h	b	s	a	l	a	m	i	w	b	m	d	h	r
p	a	t	g	r	e	l	v	i	o	x	h	a	n	b	e	t	t	m	a
s	b	u	e	b	a	g	e	l	c	d	o	t	p	a	w	z	o	o	u
r	e	p	n	z	p	o	f	x	p	o	h	e	y	c	v	e	s	s	p
s	a	l	t	r	p	i	o	y	l	f	d	f	l	o	u	r	b	o	i
b	v	h	e	r	l	y	k	l	a	m	b	u	r	n	p	h	u	n	e
h	o	o	s	t	e	c	a	v	i	h	j	w	p	f	f	o	t	y	n
m	c	o	r	n	i	p	r	r	z	y	g	a	a	h	o	k	y	p	f
l	a	e	g	t	a	k	h	g	t	x	w	i	c	a	r	r	o	t	q
k	d	h	r	d	p	o	i	s	i	a	u	o	c	d	g	v	p	o	m
z	o	e	e	k	g	r	a	p	e	f	r	u	i	t	i	o	s	m	m

vegetables	bagel	**Bonus Word**
fruit	bacon	The Bonus Word is not on the list. Find it using this hint.
pineapple	rolls	
carrot	pie	**Hint**
corn	milk	Something you put on toast or with peanut butter on a sandwich.
lamb	herbs	
shrimp	salt	
beans	grapefruit	
flour	salami	
soda	avocado	

Word Search 3 - Foods

Look at the list of words at the bottom of the page. Find these words in the boxes below. The words read forward or down. Circle each word you find and then cross it off the list. Add words you do not know to your Vocabulary Notebook at the back of the book..

l	w	h	e	a	t	o	b	s	l	m	m	d	x	v	z	i	q	f	g
d	e	j	u	v	c	k	q	b	d	l	c	o	f	e	c	a	c	o	k
y	k	a	t	r	p	e	v	m	u	i	e	n	v	o	h	s	m	f	o
l	t	o	p	a	c	h	e	e	s	e	b	u	r	g	e	r	i	m	t
o	r	t	y	p	e	o	t	r	o	b	n	t	u	c	e	w	v	a	o
h	y	e	s	r	l	x	t	r	l	h	j	x	a	i	s	o	t	s	s
s	l	h	d	e	e	v	l	r	b	a	o	m	e	l	e	t	o	o	x
a	o	n	p	c	r	c	n	n	x	r	j	m	q	o	c	s	m	b	v
l	s	f	s	o	y	i	c	a	s	h	e	w	c	w	q	y	y	l	k
m	c	w	u	i	n	h	b	o	j	s	n	e	o	w	b	m	d	h	r
o	a	t	c	r	s	a	l	a	d	x	s	u	g	a	r	t	t	m	a
n	b	u	o	n	x	k	y	i	s	d	p	t	a	n	w	z	c	o	u
r	e	p	o	z	z	o	f	x	p	o	i	e	r	e	v	e	r	s	j
p	i	c	k	l	e	i	o	y	l	f	n	y	l	o	s	t	e	a	k
b	u	j	i	l	c	y	k	w	p	m	a	u	i	c	p	h	a	n	a
l	i	m	e	t	h	c	a	v	i	h	c	w	c	f	f	o	m	y	n
m	e	c	s	s	i	p	r	r	z	y	h	a	a	h	o	k	y	p	f
l	y	e	g	t	y	o	g	u	r	t	t	i	o	e	a	o	p	b	q
k	g	h	r	d	p	o	i	s	i	a	u	o	c	d	g	v	p	o	m
z	w	w	i	n	g	s	p	r	o	t	v	g	w	a	p	p	l	e	m

sugar	lime	**Bonus Word**
cookies	celery	The Bonus Word is
omelet	spinach	not on the list. Find it
cheeseburger	garlic	using this hint.
donut	steak	
pickle	salmon	**Hint**
salad	soy	A type of nut.
cream	yogurt	
wings	cheese	
apple	wheat	

Word Search 4 - Foods

Look at the list of words at the bottom of the page. Find these words in the boxes below. The words read forward or down. Circle each word you find and then cross it off the list. Add words you do not know to your Vocabulary Notebook at the back of the book.

l	y	b	n	v	t	o	b	s	l	t	u	r	n	i	p	i	q	f	g
d	e	o	u	v	c	k	q	b	d	l	c	k	f	e	e	a	c	o	k
y	k	k	t	r	d	e	v	m	u	i	e	p	v	o	p	s	m	f	o
l	t	c	o	l	e	s	l	a	w	n	a	a	t	r	a	t	i	m	t
o	r	h	y	p	c	o	t	r	o	b	l	e	m	o	n	w	v	a	j
h	y	o	s	r	a	x	t	r	l	h	j	x	a	i	c	o	t	s	u
s	l	y	d	e	f	v	l	r	b	a	p	s	q	u	a	s	h	o	i
t	o	n	p	c	r	c	n	n	x	r	j	m	q	o	k	s	m	b	c
i	h	o	t	d	o	g	b	o	c	a	b	b	a	g	e	y	y	l	e
m	c	w	u	i	n	h	b	o	j	s	n	e	o	w	s	m	d	h	r
p	e	p	p	e	r	l	v	h	a	m	h	a	n	t	e	t	t	m	a
o	b	u	e	n	x	k	y	i	s	d	o	t	p	n	w	z	o	o	u
t	e	p	c	l	a	m	s	x	p	o	h	e	t	o	m	a	t	o	j
a	t	g	t	r	i	i	o	y	l	f	d	y	w	o	e	a	u	o	w
t	u	j	e	l	c	y	k	w	c	h	i	c	k	e	n	h	i	n	a
o	d	o	s	t	h	c	a	v	a	h	j	w	p	f	f	o	c	y	n
e	m	m	e	l	o	n	r	r	k	y	g	a	a	c	h	i	l	i	f
s	y	e	g	t	a	k	h	g	e	x	w	i	o	e	a	o	p	b	q
k	g	h	r	d	p	o	i	s	i	a	u	o	c	d	g	v	p	o	m
z	c	u	c	u	m	b	e	r	o	t	v	g	w	o	r	a	n	g	e

		Bonus Word
orange	pancakes	The Bonus Word is not on the list. Find it using this hint.
melon	coleslaw	
cabbage	bok choy	
turnip	pepper	
potatoes	juice	**Hint**
ham	cucumber	A red colored spice.
chicken	decaf	Also, a flavorful stew.
clams	lemon	
cake	tomato	
hotdog	squash	

Word Search 5 - Foods

Look at the list of words at the bottom of the page. Find these words in the boxes below. The words read forward or down. Circle each word you find and then cross it off the list. Add words you do not know to your Vocabulary Notebook at the back of the book.

r	a	i	s	i	n	o	b	s	s	m	m	p	m	v	z	i	q	f	t
a	e	j	u	v	c	k	q	b	a	l	c	k	u	e	e	a	c	o	u
s	k	a	t	r	p	e	v	m	u	i	e	p	s	o	s	s	m	f	n
p	t	o	m	a	y	o	a	f	s	p	a	g	h	e	t	t	i	m	a
b	r	t	y	p	e	o	t	r	a	b	n	t	r	c	u	w	v	a	f
e	y	e	s	r	y	x	t	r	g	h	j	x	o	i	f	o	t	s	i
r	l	h	b	r	o	w	n	i	e	a	p	j	o	z	f	p	o	o	s
r	o	n	p	c	r	c	n	n	x	r	j	m	m	o	i	s	m	b	h
i	s	c	h	a	i	x	b	t	e	a	e	t	s	w	n	y	l	l	k
e	c	w	u	i	n	h	b	o	j	s	n	e	o	w	g	m	o	h	r
s	c	a	l	l	i	o	n	i	o	x	h	a	n	t	e	t	b	m	a
s	b	u	e	n	x	k	y	d	r	u	m	s	t	i	c	k	s	o	u
r	e	b	n	z	z	o	f	x	p	o	h	e	y	e	v	e	t	s	j
a	t	r	t	r	w	i	o	y	l	f	d	y	w	o	e	a	e	o	w
b	u	o	e	l	a	y	k	p	u	n	c	h	r	c	p	h	r	n	a
h	d	c	s	t	f	c	a	v	i	h	j	w	p	f	f	o	t	y	n
m	e	c	j	s	f	p	r	r	z	y	g	p	o	p	s	i	c	l	e
l	y	o	g	t	l	k	k	i	w	i	w	i	o	e	a	o	p	b	q
k	g	l	r	d	e	o	i	s	i	a	c	h	o	c	o	l	a	t	e
z	m	i	l	k	s	h	a	k	e	t	v	g	w	b	i	o	s	m	m

		Bonus Word
raspberries	popsicle	The Bonus Word is not on the list. Find it using this hint.
raisin	milkshake	
broccoli	sausage	
scallion	waffles	
mushrooms	punch	
drumsticks	spaghetti	**Hint**
tunafish	brownie	A type of tea.
lobster	tea	
chocolate	mayo	
stuffing	kiwi	

15

Find the Letter 1 – Foods

Goal: Find the Letter puzzles help you recognize and learn new words.

Pick a letter to go into the empty box on each line to make a word. The letter may be at the beginning, in the middle or at the end of the word. You can only use a letter one time. Add words you do not know to your Vocabulary Notebook. The first word, *roast*, is an example.

a	b	c	d	e	f	g	h	i	j	k	l	m	n	o	p	q	r	s	t	u	v	w	x	y	z

f	u	s	v	r	**o**	a	s	t	m	a
s	w	o	r	d		i	s	h	y	w
t	o	m	e	f		g	s	c	j	i
r	e	e	g	g		l	a	n	t	o
l	s	y	b	w		e	e	t	s	n
k	e	o	y	s		e	r	s	b	u
i	p	a	r	s		e	y	u	f	h
v	e	a	l	c		t	l	e	t	s
o	i	a	t	p		a	s	k	m	c

Find the Letter 2 - Foods

Pick a letter to go into the empty box on each line to make a word. The letter may be at the beginning, in the middle or at the end of the word. You can only use a letter one time. Add words you do not know to your Vocabulary Notebook at the back of the book.

| a | b | c | d | e | f | g | h | i | j | k | l | m | n | o | p | q | r | s | t | u | v | w | x | y | z |

s	c	a	n	d		b	a	r	m	g
f	w	o	o	i		i	s	o	a	e
j	c	h	i	c		p	e	a	s	o
i	c	e	c	r		a	m	n	t	g
t	s	y	r	a		i	s	h	s	n
d	t	o	y	s		h	e	r	r	y
p	p	a	m	a		g	o	u	f	b
q	e	p	c	r		c	k	e	r	i
i	c	t	o	r		i	l	l	a	s

Find the Letter 3 – Foods

Pick a letter to go into the empty box on each line to make a word. The letter may be at the beginning, in the middle or at the end of the word. You can only use a letter one time. Add words you do not know to your Vocabulary Notebook at the back of the book.

a	b	c	d	e	f	g	h	i	j	k	l	m	n	o	p	q	r	s	t	u	v	w	x	y	z

y	c	a	n	p		u	n	e	s	f
p	n	e	c	t		r	i	n	e	t
o	c	h	i	x		o	d	a	s	w
r	c	e	r	i		s	m	n	t	y
c	a	u	l	i		l	o	w	e	r
t	r	o	n	o		d	l	e	s	n
f	l	a	s	a		n	a	o	f	d
a	l	m	o	n		s	e	r	h	u
h	c	t	l	i		e	r	l	a	r

19

Find the Letter 4 – Grocery Store Words

Pick a letter to go into the empty box on each line to make a word. The letter may be at the beginning, in the middle or at the end of the word. You can only use a letter one time. Add words you do not know to your Vocabulary Notebook at the back of the book. **These are words found in a grocery store where you buy food.** Think about the different sections found in a grocery store.

a	b	c	d	e	f	g	h	i	j	k	l	m	n	o	p	q	r	s	t	u	v	w	x	y	z

o	j	a	d	e		i	a	r	d	m
g	p	i	o	i		e	a	t	a	a
k	s	u	m	d		i	r	y	i	a
f	r	o	z	e		f	o	o	d	s
c	b	y	r	s		a	f	o	o	d
h	t	g	p	o		l	t	r	y	b
p	b	e	v	e		a	g	e	s	o
b	a	k	e	r		k	e	r	k	x
e	s	n	a	c		s	e	i	s	e

Find the Letter 5 – Restaurant Words

Pick a letter to go into the empty box on each line to make a word. The letter may be at the beginning, in the middle or at the end of the word. You can only use a letter one time. Add words you do not know to your Vocabulary Notebook at the back of the book. **These are words found on a restaurant menu.**

a	b	c	d	e	f	g	h	i	j	k	l	m	n	o	p	q	r	s	t	u	v	w	x	y	z

m	c	s	p	e		i	a	l	s	y
d	m	a	i	n		i	s	h	e	s
b	n	d	r	i		k	s	m	s	e
v	d	r	e	s		i	n	g	s	o
o	s	s	a	l		d	s	r	g	a
w	s	a	n	d		i	c	h	e	s
d	e	s	s	e		t	s	t	o	e
x	e	s	h	s		d	e	s	h	h
k	i	d	d	i		m	e	a	l	s

21

Letters to Words Unscramble

Goal: Recognize and learn new words and their correct spelling. Use words in a sentence.

Unscramble the letters to make a food word. First, write the word on the line next to the scrambled letters. Then, write a sentence using the word on the line below. Words that you do not know the meaning of, add to your Vocabulary Notebook at the back of this book.

There is a word list for these word puzzles at the end of this section. Use this list if you have a difficult time completing one of these puzzles. The first word is done for you as an example.

1. Lirshe - _relish_

   I like mustard and relish on a hotdog.
   _____

2. ppaizrete - _____

   _____

3. ssdetre _____

   _____

4. eenret _____

   _____

5. chpketu _____

   _____

6. rdmutas _____

   _____

7. realce _____

   _____

8. iemoosht _____

_____

9. etalt _____

_____

10. ropdcue _____

_____

11. alnmdeoe _____

_____

12. labmteals _____

_____

13. ypoutrl _____

_____

14. rsou mrcea _____   _____

_____

15. ttcoaeg cesehe _____   _____

_____

16. llbe rpepep _____   _____

_____

17. ndgoru fbee _____ _____

_____

18. thwie bdrea _____ _____

_____

19. dscbrmale ggse _____ _____

_____

20. fceh daals _____ _____

_____

21. tho clooatehc _____ _____

_____

22. dcie ate _____ _____

_____

23. plema psryu _____ _____

_____

24. gle of mbla _____ _____ _____

_____

25. cam nda eeesch _____ _____ _____

_____

Letters to Words Unscramble – Word List

Here is a word list for the Letters to Words puzzles. This list is in alphabetical order. Look at this list if you have a difficult time completing one of these Letters to Words puzzles. The answer for the first bunch of letters, relish, is not included in this list.

1. appetizer
2. bell pepper
3. cereal
4. chef salad
5. cottage cheese
6. dessert
7. entree
8. ground beef
9. hot chocolate
10. iced tea
11. ketchup
12. latte
13. leg of lamb
14. lemonade
15. mac and cheese
16. maple syrup
17. meatballs
18. mustard
19. poultry
20. produce
21. scrambled eggs
22. smoothie
23. sour cream
24. white bread

Phrase Match

Goal: Recognize and learn everyday food phrases.

Use the word list below to pick a word or words to go with the correct phrase. The number after each phrase tells you how many words go with that phrase. Cross out each word as you use it. You can use a word only one time. The first phrase, *A head of*, has been started for you.

~~lettuce~~	parsley	eggs	water	wine
crackers	bread	cheese	jelly	butter
mayonnaise	ice cream	bacon	cookies	gum
oil	yogurt	soup	chips	cabbage
salt	whip cream	cereal	tea	celery

A head of (2)	A carton of (1)	A bottle of (1)	A package of (1)	A loaf of (1)
lettuce				
A stalk of (1)	**A dollop of (1)**	**A box of (2)**	**A pack of (1)**	
A scoop of (1)	**A jar of (2)**	**A stick of (1)**	**A slab of (1)**	
A container of (1)	**A drizzle of (1)**	**A dash of (1)**	**A block of (1)**	
A cup of (1)	**A bunch of (1)**	**A bag of (1)**	**A glass of (1)**	

28

Learning New Words

Master Food Word List

This is a list of food words used in this puzzle book. Write the definition for each word. Words you do not know add to your *Vocabulary Notebook* and then look up the meaning of the word.

Word	Definition
appetizer	
apple	
avocado	
bacon	
bagel	
banana	
beans	
beef	
bell pepper	
bok choy	
broccoli	
brownie	
butter	
cabbage	
cake	
carrot	
catfish	

Food Word List, continued

Word	Definition
celery	
cereal	
cheese	
cheeseburger	
chef salad	
chicken	
chocolate	
chowder	
clams	
coffee	
coleslaw	
cookies	
corn	
cottage cheese	
cream	
cucumber	
decaf	
dessert	
donut	

Food Word List, continued

Word	Definition
drumsticks	
eggs	
entrée	
flour	
fries	
fruit	
garlic	
grapefruit	
ground beef	
ham	
hamburger	
herbs	
hot chocolate	
hot dog	
iced tea	
juice	
ketchup	
kiwi	

Food Word List, continued

Word	Definition
lamb	
latte	
leg of lamb	
lemon	
lemonade	
lettuce	
lime	
lobster	
mac and cheese	
maple syrup	
margarine	
mayo	
meatballs	
melon	
milk	
milkshake	
muffin	
mushrooms	
mustard	

Food Word List, continued

Word	Definition
nuts	
olives	
omelet	
onion	
orange	
pancakes	
pasta	
pepper	
peppers	
pickle	
pie	
pineapple	
pizza	
popsicle	
potatoes	
poultry	
produce	
punch	
raisin	

Food Word List, continued

Word	Definition
raspberries	
relish	
rice	
rolls	
salad	
salami	
salmon	
salt	
sausage	
scallion	
scrambled eggs	
shrimp	
smoothie	
soda	
soup	
sour cream	
soy	
spaghetti	
spinach	

Food Word List, continued

Word	Definition
squash	
steak	
stuffing	
sugar	
tea	
toast	
tomato	
tunafish	
turkey	
turnip	
vegetables	
waffles	
wheat	
white bread	
wings	
yogurt	

Grocery Store Words

Word	Definition
bakery	
beverages	
dairy	
deli	
frozen foods	
meat	
poultry	
seafood	
snacks	

Restaurant Words (Menu)

Word	Definition
desserts	
dressings	
drinks	
kiddie meals	
main dishes	
salads	
sandwiches	
sides	
specials	

Words to Learn List

Write the words you do not know here. Take a guess and write what you think the word means before you look it up in a dictionary.

Words to Learn	What I think the word means	Word Definition

Words to Learn List, continued

Words to Learn	What I think the word means	Word Definition

How to Create a Vocabulary Notebook

Making a vocabulary notebook is a good way to learn and remember new English words. Here is what you do.

1. Write the word you want to learn. (in English)
2. Write the word in your native language.
3. Write the definition of the word or phrase. (in English)
4. Write a sentence using the word or phrase. (in English)

Example:

Word to learn: _____ *remember* _____

Word in my native language: _____ *recorder (using Spanish for example)*

Word definition: _____ *To bring to mind, recall.* _____

Word in a sentence:

_____ *I will remember to write new words in my Vocabulary Notebook.* _____

Word to learn: _____

Word in my native language: _____

Word definition: _____

_____

Word in a sentence:

_____

Word to learn: _____

Word in my native language: _____

Word definition: _____

_____

Word in a sentence:

_____

Vocabulary Notebook, continued

Word to learn: _____

Word in my native language: _____

Word definition: _____

_____

Word in a sentence:

_____

Word to learn: _____

Word in my native language: _____

Word definition: _____

_____

Word in a sentence:

_____

Word to learn: _____

Word in my native language: _____

Word definition: _____

_____

Word in a sentence:

_____

Word to learn: _____

Word in my native language: _____

Word definition: _____

_____

Word in a sentence:

_____

Vocabulary Notebook, continued

Word to learn: _____

Word in my native language: _____

Word definition: _____

_____

Word in a sentence:

_____

Word to learn: _____

Word in my native language: _____

Word definition: _____

_____

Word in a sentence:

_____

Word to learn: _____

Word in my native language: _____

Word definition: _____

_____

Word in a sentence:

_____

Word to learn: _____

Word in my native language: _____

Word definition: _____

_____

Word in a sentence:

_____

Vocabulary Notebook, continued

Word to learn: _____

Word in my native language: _____

Word definition: _____

_____

Word in a sentence:

_____

Word to learn: _____

Word in my native language: _____

Word definition: _____

_____

Word in a sentence:

_____

Word to learn: _____

Word in my native language: _____

Word definition: _____

_____

Word in a sentence:

_____

Word to learn: _____

Word in my native language: _____

Word definition: _____

_____

Word in a sentence:

_____

Vocabulary Notebook, continued

Word to learn: _____

Word in my native language: _____

Word definition: _____

_____

Word in a sentence:

_____

Word to learn: _____

Word in my native language: _____

Word definition: _____

_____

Word in a sentence:

_____

Word to learn: _____

Word in my native language: _____

Word definition: _____

_____

Word in a sentence:

_____

Word to learn: _____

Word in my native language: _____

Word definition: _____

_____

Word in a sentence:

_____

Vocabulary Notebook, continued

Word to learn: _____

Word in my native language: _____

Word definition: _____

_____

Word in a sentence:

_____

Word to learn: _____

Word in my native language: _____

Word definition: _____

_____

Word in a sentence:

_____

Word to learn: _____

Word in my native language: _____

Word definition: _____

_____

Word in a sentence:

_____

Word to learn: _____

Word in my native language: _____

Word definition: _____

_____

Word in a sentence:

_____

Pronunciation Page

Here is what you can do to practice English speaking and pronunciation.

1. Write the words or phrases you want to learn to pronounce below the line.
2. Go to the Internet and find an online dictionary or search engine.
3. Look up the word and select an option that let's you hear how the word is pronounced.
4. Practice repeating and saying the word.
5. Or, ask someone you know how to say the word. Practice your pronunciation with this person.

Write the words or phrases you want to learn how to pronounce here.

Pronunciation Page, continued

Write the words or phrases you want to learn how to pronounce here. Then, ask someone to help you learn how to say these words. Or, go an online dictionary to listen to how the word is pronounced.

Answer Section

Word Search 1 – Answers

b	u	t	t	e	r	o	b	s	l	m	m	p	c	v	z	i	q	f	e
v	k	j	u	v	c	k	q	b	d	l	c	s	o	u	p	a	c	o	g
y	k	a	t	r	o	n	i	o	n	b	e	p	f	o	p	s	m	f	g
l	t	o	p	a	s	t	a	f	u	n	a	a	f	r	r	t	i	m	s
o	r	t	y	p	e	o	t	r	t	b	n	t	e	c	p	w	v	a	o
l	y	o	l	i	v	e	s	g	s	h	j	p	e	p	p	e	r	s	s
e	l	h	d	e	i	v	l	r	b	a	p	j	w	z	n	p	i	o	x
t	o	n	p	c	r	b	n	n	x	r	h	m	q	o	c	s	c	b	v
t	s	f	h	k	m	a	i	o	n	y	a	t	c	w	q	y	e	l	m
u	c	w	u	i	n	n	b	o	j	s	m	e	o	w	b	m	d	h	a
c	a	t	f	r	e	a	v	i	o	x	b	e	e	f	e	t	t	m	r
e	b	u	r	n	x	n	y	i	s	d	u	t	p	n	w	z	o	o	g
r	e	p	i	z	z	a	f	x	p	o	r	u	y	r	v	e	s	s	a
a	t	g	e	r	i	n	o	y	l	f	g	y	w	o	e	a	b	o	r
b	u	j	s	l	c	y	k	w	p	m	e	u	r	c	p	h	u	n	i
h	d	o	o	t	c	h	o	w	d	e	r	w	p	m	u	f	f	i	n
m	e	c	j	s	i	p	r	r	z	y	b	a	a	h	o	k	y	p	e
l	t	u	r	k	e	y	h	g	t	x	w	i	o	e	a	o	p	b	e
k	g	h	r	d	p	o	i	s	i	a	u	o	c	d	g	v	p	o	m
z	w	e	e	k	p	r	t	o	a	s	t	g	w	b	i	o	s	m	l

		Bonus Word
butter	turkey	
onion	lettuce	muffin
pasta	peppers	
soup	beef	
coffee	pizza	
chowder	rice	
toast	banana	
eggs	nuts	
hamburger	margarine	
fries	olives	

Word Search 2 – Answers

l	y	p	n	v	t	o	b	v	l	m	m	p	x	h	e	r	b	s	g
d	e	j	u	v	c	k	q	e	d	l	c	k	f	e	e	a	c	o	k
y	k	a	t	r	p	e	v	g	u	i	e	p	v	o	p	s	m	f	o
l	s	o	m	a	s	t	a	e	g	n	j	a	t	r	s	t	i	m	t
o	h	t	i	p	e	o	t	o	b	e	t	u	c	o	w	v	a	o	
h	r	o	l	l	s	x	t	a	l	h	l	x	a	i	d	o	t	s	s
s	i	h	k	e	i	v	l	b	b	a	l	j	b	e	a	n	s	o	x
t	m	n	p	c	p	c	n	l	x	r	y	m	q	o	c	s	m	b	v
i	p	f	h	k	i	b	e	u	t	e	t	c	w	f	r	u	i	t	
m	c	w	u	i	n	h	b	s	a	l	a	m	i	w	b	m	d	h	r
p	a	t	g	r	e	l	v	i	o	x	h	a	n	b	e	t	t	m	a
s	b	u	e	b	a	g	e	l	s	d	o	t	p	a	w	z	o	o	u
r	e	p	n	z	p	o	f	x	p	o	h	e	y	c	v	e	s	s	p
s	a	l	t	r	p	i	o	y	l	f	d	f	l	o	u	r	b	o	i
b	v	h	e	r	l	y	k	l	a	m	b	u	r	n	p	h	u	n	e
h	o	o	s	t	e	c	a	v	i	h	j	w	p	f	f	o	t	y	n
m	c	o	r	n	i	p	r	r	z	y	g	a	a	h	o	k	y	p	f
l	a	e	g	t	a	k	h	g	t	x	w	i	c	a	r	r	o	t	q
k	d	h	r	d	p	o	i	s	i	a	u	o	c	d	g	v	p	o	m
z	o	e	e	k	g	r	a	p	e	f	r	u	i	t	i	o	s	m	m

		Bonus Word
vegetables	bagel	
fruit	bacon	
pineapple	rolls	jelly
carrot	pie	
corn	milk	
lamb	herbs	
shrimp	salt	
beans	grapefruit	
flour	salami	
soda	avocado	

Word Search 3 – Answers

l	w	h	e	a	t	o	b	s	l	m	m	d	x	v	z	i	q	f	g
d	e	j	u	v	c	k	q	b	d	l	c	o	f	e	c	a	c	o	k
y	k	a	t	r	p	e	v	m	u	i	e	n	v	o	h	s	m	f	o
l	t	o	p	a	c	h	e	e	s	e	b	u	r	g	e	r	i	m	t
o	r	t	y	p	e	o	t	r	o	b	n	t	u	c	e	w	v	a	o
h	y	e	s	r	l	x	t	r	l	h	j	x	a	i	s	o	t	s	s
s	l	h	d	e	e	v	l	r	b	a	o	m	e	l	e	t	o	o	x
a	o	n	p	c	r	c	n	n	x	r	j	m	q	o	c	s	m	b	v
l	s	f	s	o	y	i	c	a	s	h	e	w	c	w	q	y	y	l	k
m	c	w	u	i	n	h	b	o	j	s	n	e	o	w	b	m	d	h	r
o	a	t	c	r	s	a	l	a	d	x	s	u	g	a	r	t	t	m	a
n	b	u	o	n	x	k	y	i	s	d	p	t	a	n	w	z	c	o	u
r	e	p	o	z	z	o	f	x	p	o	i	e	r	e	v	e	r	s	j
p	i	c	k	l	e	i	o	y	l	f	n	y	l	o	s	t	e	a	k
b	u	j	i	l	c	y	k	w	p	m	a	u	i	c	p	h	a	n	a
l	i	m	e	t	h	c	a	v	i	h	c	w	c	f	f	o	m	y	n
m	e	c	s	s	i	p	r	r	z	y	h	a	a	h	o	k	y	p	f
l	y	e	g	t	y	o	g	u	r	t	b	i	o	e	a	o	p	b	q
k	g	h	r	d	p	o	i	s	i	a	u	o	c	d	g	v	p	o	m
z	w	w	i	n	g	s	p	r	o	t	v	g	w	a	p	p	l	e	m

		Bonus Word
sugar	lime	
cookies	celery	cashew
omelet	spinach	
cheeseburger	garlic	
donut	steak	
pickle	salmon	
salad	soy	
cream	yogurt	
wings	cheese	
apple	wheat	

Word Search 4 – Answers

l	y	**b**	n	v	t	o	b	s	l	**t**	u	**r**	n	**i**	p	i	q	f	**g**
d	e	**o**	u	v	c	k	q	b	d	l	c	k	f	e	e	a	c	o	k
y	k	**k**	t	r	**d**	e	v	m	u	i	e	p	v	o	**p**	s	m	f	o
l	t	**c**	**o**	**l**	**e**	**s**	**l**	**a**	**w**	n	a	a	t	r	**a**	t	i	m	t
o	r	**h**	y	p	**c**	o	t	r	o	b	**l**	**e**	**m**	**o**	**n**	w	v	a	**j**
h	y	**o**	s	r	**a**	x	t	r	l	h	j	x	a	i	**c**	o	t	s	**u**
s	l	**y**	d	e	**f**	v	l	r	b	a	p	**s**	**q**	**u**	**a**	**s**	**h**	o	**i**
t	o	n	p	c	r	c	n	n	x	r	j	m	q	o	**k**	s	m	b	**c**
i	**h**	**o**	**t**	**d**	**o**	**g**	b	o	**c**	**a**	**b**	**b**	**a**	**g**	**e**	y	y	l	**e**
m	c	w	u	i	n	h	b	o	j	s	n	e	o	w	**s**	m	d	h	r
p	**e**	**p**	**p**	**e**	**r**	l	v	**h**	**a**	**m**	h	a	n	t	e	t	t	m	a
o	b	u	e	n	x	k	y	i	s	d	o	t	p	n	w	z	o	o	u
t	e	p	**c**	**l**	**a**	**m**	**s**	x	p	o	h	e	**t**	**o**	**m**	**a**	**t**	**o**	j
a	t	g	t	r	i	i	o	y	l	f	d	y	w	o	e	a	k	o	w
t	u	j	e	l	c	y	k	w	**c**	**h**	**i**	**c**	**k**	**e**	**n**	h	i	n	a
o	d	o	s	t	h	c	a	v	**a**	h	j	w	p	f	f	o	p	y	n
e	m	**m**	**e**	**l**	**o**	**n**	r	r	**k**	y	g	a	a	**c**	**h**	**i**	**l**	**i**	f
s	y	e	g	t	a	k	h	g	**e**	x	w	i	o	e	a	o	p	b	q
k	g	h	r	d	p	o	i	s	i	a	u	o	c	d	g	v	p	o	m
z	**c**	**u**	**c**	**u**	**m**	**b**	**e**	**r**	o	t	v	g	w	**o**	**r**	**a**	**n**	**g**	**e**

		Bonus Word
orange	pancakes	
melon	coleslaw	
cabbage	bok choy	chili
turnip	pepper	
potatoes	juice	
ham	cucumber	
chicken	decaf	
clams	lemon	
cake	tomato	
hotdog	squash	

Word Search 5 – Answers

r	**a**	**i**	**s**	**i**	**n**	o	b	s	**s**	m	m	p	**m**	v	z	i	q	f	**t**
a	e	j	u	v	c	k	q	b	**a**	l	c	k	**u**	e	e	a	c	o	**u**
s	k	a	t	r	p	e	v	m	**u**	i	e	p	**s**	o	s	s	m	f	**n**
p	t	o	**m**	**a**	**y**	**o**	a	f	**s**	**p**	a	**g**	**h**	**e**	**t**	**t**	i	m	**a**
b	r	t	y	p	e	o	t	r	a	b	n	t	**r**	c	**u**	w	v	a	**f**
e	y	e	s	r	y	x	t	r	**g**	h	j	x	**o**	i	**f**	o	t	s	**i**
r	l	h	**b**	**r**	**o**	**w**	**n**	i	**e**	a	p	j	**o**	z	**f**	p	o	o	**s**
r	o	n	p	c	r	c	n	n	x	r	j	m	**m**	o	i	s	m	b	**h**
i	s	**c**	**h**	**a**	**i**	x	b	**t**	e	**a**	e	t	**s**	w	n	y	l	l	k
e	c	w	u	i	n	h	b	**o**	j	s	n	e	**o**	w	**g**	m	**o**	h	r
s	**c**	**a**	**l**	**l**	**i**	**o**	**n**	i	o	x	h	a	n	t	e	t	**b**	m	a
s	b	u	e	n	x	k	y	**d**	**r**	**u**	**m**	**s**	**t**	**i**	**c**	**k**	**s**	o	u
r	e	**b**	n	z	z	o	f	x	p	o	h	e	y	e	v	e	**t**	s	j
a	t	**r**	t	r	**w**	i	o	y	l	f	d	y	w	o	e	a	**e**	o	w
b	u	**o**	e	l	**a**	y	k	**p**	**u**	**n**	**c**	**h**	r	c	p	h	**r**	n	a
h	d	**c**	s	t	**f**	c	a	v	i	h	j	w	p	f	f	o	t	y	n
m	e	**c**	j	s	**f**	p	r	r	z	y	g	**p**	**o**	**p**	**s**	**i**	**c**	**l**	**e**
l	y	**o**	g	t	l	k	**k**	**i**	**w**	**i**	w	i	o	e	a	o	p	b	q
k	g	**l**	r	d	**e**	o	i	s	i	a	**c**	**h**	**o**	**c**	**o**	**l**	**a**	**t**	**e**
z	**m**	**i**	**l**	**k**	**s**	**h**	**a**	**k**	**e**	t	v	g	w	b	i	o	s	m	m

		Bonus Word
raspberries	popsicle	
raisin	milkshake	
broccoli	sausage	chai
scallion	waffles	
mushrooms	punch	
drumsticks	spaghetti	
tunafish	brownie	
lobster	tea	
chocolate	mayo	
stuffing	kiwi	

Find the Letter 1 - Answers

f	u	s	v	r	o	a	s	t	m	a
s	w	o	r	d	f	i	s	h	y	w
t	o	m	e	f	i	g	s	c	j	i
r	e	e	g	g	p	l	a	n	t	o
l	s	y	b	w	b	e	e	t	s	n
k	e	o	y	s	t	e	r	s	b	u
i	p	a	r	s	l	e	y	u	f	h
v	e	a	l	c	u	t	l	e	t	s
o	i	a	t	p	e	a	s	k	m	c

Find the Letter 2 - Answers

s	c	a	n	d	y	b	a	r	m	g
f	w	o	o	i	l	i	s	o	a	e
j	c	h	i	c	k	p	e	a	s	o
i	c	e	c	r	e	a	m	n	t	g
t	s	y	r	a	d	i	s	h	s	n
d	t	o	y	s	c	h	e	r	r	y
p	p	a	m	a	n	g	o	u	f	b
q	e	x	c	r	a	c	k	e	r	i
i	c	t	o	r	t	i	l	l	a	s

Find the Letter 3 – Answers

y	c	a	n	p	**r**	u	n	e	s	f
p	n	e	c	t	**a**	r	i	n	e	t
o	c	h	i	x	**c**	o	d	a	s	w
r	c	e	r	i	**b**	s	m	n	t	y
c	a	u	l	i	**f**	l	o	w	e	r
t	r	o	n	o	**o**	d	l	e	s	n
f	l	a	s	a	**g**	n	a	o	f	d
a	l	m	o	n	**d**	s	e	r	h	u
h	c	t	l	i	**v**	e	r	l	a	r

Find the Letter 4 – Grocery Store Words

o	j	a	d	e	l	i	a	r	d	m
g	p	i	o	i	m	e	a	t	a	a
k	s	u	m	d	a	i	r	y	i	a
f	r	o	z	e	n	f	o	o	d	s
c	b	y	r	s	e	a	f	o	o	d
h	t	g	p	o	u	l	t	r	y	b
p	b	e	v	e	r	a	g	e	s	o
b	a	k	e	r	y	k	e	r	k	x
e	s	n	a	c	k	s	e	i	s	e

Find the Letter 5 – Restaurant Words

m	c	s	p	e	c	i	a	l	s	y
d	m	a	i	n	d	i	s	h	e	s
b	n	d	r	i	n	k	s	m	s	e
v	d	r	e	s	s	i	n	g	s	o
o	s	s	a	l	a	d	s	r	g	a
w	s	a	n	d	w	i	c	h	e	s
d	e	s	s	e	r	t	s	t	o	e
x	e	s	h	s	i	d	e	s	h	h
k	i	d	d	i	e	m	e	a	l	s

Letters to Words - Answers

1. lirshe - relish
2. ppaizrete - appetizer
3. ssdetre - dessert
4. eenret - entree
5. chpketu - ketchup
6. rdmutas - mustard
7. realce - cereal
8. iemoosht - smoothie
9. etalt - latte
10. ropdcue - produce
11. alnmdeoe - lemonade
12. labmteals - meatballs
13. ypoutrl - poultry
14. rsou mrcea – sour cream
15. ttcoaeg cesehe – cottage cheese
16. llbe rpepep – bell pepper
17. ndgoru fbee – ground beef
18. thwie bdrea – white bread
19. dscbrmale ggse – scrambled eggs
20. fceh daals – chef salad
21. tho clooatehc – hot chocolate
22. dcie ate – iced tea
23. plema psryu – maple syrup
24. gle of mbla – leg of lamb
25. cam nda eeesch – mac and cheese

Phrase Match - Answers

Word list

lettuce	parsley	eggs	water	wine
crackers	bread	cheese	jelly	butter
mayonnaise	ice cream	bacon	cookies	gum
oil	yogurt	soup	chips	cabbage
salt	whip cream	cereal	tea	celery

A head of (2) lettuce cabbage	A carton of (1) eggs	A bottle of (1) water (or wine)	A package of (1) cookies	A loaf of (1) bread
A stalk of (1) celery	A dollop of (1) whip cream	A box of (2) crackers cereal	A pack of (1) gum	
A scoop of (1) ice cream	A jar of (2) jelly mayonnaise	A stick of (1) butter	A slab of (1) bacon	
A container of (1) yogurt	A drizzle of (1) oil	A dash of (1) salt	A block of (1) cheese	
A cup of (1) tea	A bunch of (1) parsley	A bag of (1) chips	A glass of (1) wine (or water)	

My Notes

My Notes

Books by Kathy Nosal

English as a Second Language (ESL)

The Little Guide for the New ESL Teacher

Just One Topic ESL Word Puzzles – Food

Aging

The Adult Child's Guide to Planning Your Aging Parents' Move

Bible Study

The Not-So-Impossible Book of Revelation

www.ingramcontent.com/pod-product-compliance
Lightning Source LLC
Chambersburg PA
CBHW080530030426
42337CB00023B/4683